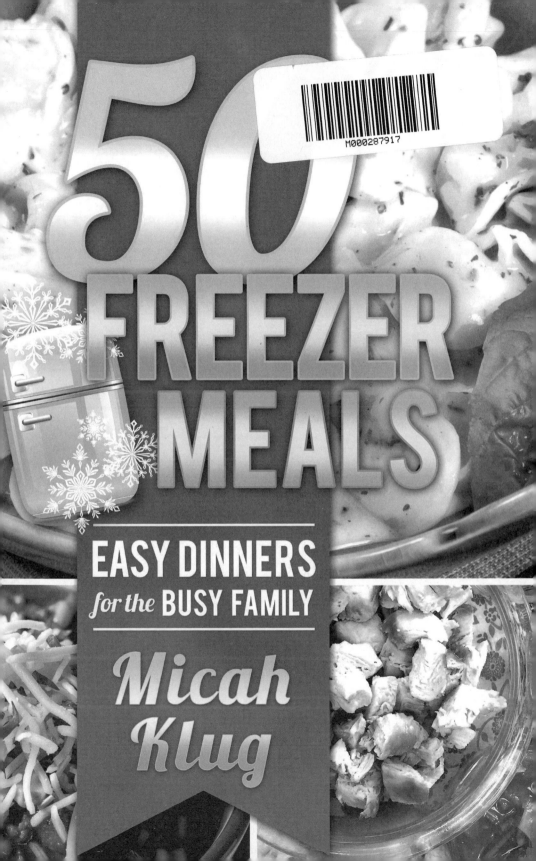

50 FREEZER MEALS

EASY DINNERS
for the BUSY FAMILY

Micah Klug

50 FREEZER MEALS

EASY DINNERS
for the BUSY FAMILY

Micah Klug

Front Table Books
an imprint of Cedar Fort, Inc.
Springville, Utah

ISBN 13: 978-1-4621-1781-9

Published by Front Table Books, an imprint of Cedar Fort, Inc.
2373 W. 700 S., Springville, UT 84663
Distributed by Cedar Fort, Inc., www.cedarfort.com

LIBRARY OF CONGRESS CATALOGING-IN-PUBLICATION DATA
Klug, Micah, 1985- author.
50 freezer meals : easy dinners for the busy family / Micah Klug.
    pages cm
Includes index.
ISBN 978-1-4621-1781-9 (perfect bound : acid-free paper)
1. Ready meals. I. Title. II. Title: Fifty freezer meals.
TX833.5.K56 2015
641.5--dc23
                    2015033388

Cover design by Rebecca J. Greenwood
Cover design © 2016 by Cedar Fort, Inc.
Edited and typeset by Sydnee Hyer

Printed in the United States of America

10 9 8 7 6 5 4 3 2 1

Printed on acid-free paper

*To my sweetheart, Travis. Thank you for
your patience, support, and love.*

*To our little ones, may heaven's blessing
be with each of you.*

Contents

CONTENTS

OTHER   93

SNEAK PEEK INTO BREAKFAST FREEZER MEALS   105

INDEX   113

ABOUT THE AUTHOR   117

DATE:

CONTENTS: CROCKPOT CKN+
DUMPLINGS

LOW 8 HRS

-DD BISCUITS TO
CROCKPOT 1 HR
BEFORE SERVING
(SHRED CKN).

Introduction

I never understood the value of freezer meals until after I had my first child. After all the hustle and bustle of family members and friends coming over to help cook and clean, I realized that, once everyone left, life was now the three of us. Like most young mothers, I experienced the newfound struggle of trying to tend to the new baby's needs, my spouse, and the household chores (among other things), and as such, dinners would often be placed on the back burner. We found ourselves eating (a lot of) easy and quick meals (fast food, top ramen, mac and cheese, peanut butter and jelly sandwiches . . . feel like a college student again, anyone?).

When we found out we were expecting our second child, we vividly remembered the struggle of recovering from the delivery, the overwhelming feeling of finding a new norm, and the new challenges of once again establishing balance. My husband and I sat down after tucking our rambunctious toddler into bed one night and discussed what made life especially easier those first few weeks. And the first thing that came to mind? Food.

We then spent a portion of the second pregnancy finding freezer meal recipes we could make, store properly, and eat. We were thrilled to know we would have these meals to eat after our extended family returned to their homes from helping with the newborn. Recipes that were not only healthy and easy to make, but amazingly delicious. Meals we looked forward to eating. After making our grocery list and coming home from vanquishing several aisles in the grocery store, we spent one solid Saturday preparing and making these freezer meals.

After our second child was born and family began to leave, having these freezer meals was our saving grace. The meals lasted for months safely in the freezer and cooked as if we had made them that day. The purpose of this recipe book is to provide simple but delicious meals that anyone can make from everyday ingredients, while also providing the freezing instructions and preparation guide. We hope you enjoy the recipes in this cookbook and the help this book can give. Good luck and happy cooking.

THE KLUG FAMILY

Tips and Tricks

Preparing freezer meals will make dinners easy, but having the proper resources will make this endeavor even easier.

MUST-HAVE SUPPLIES

• **A PERMANENT MARKER FOR PROPER LABELING.** Label the meal's name, the baking instructions, and the date to be consumed by. This will make for easy and stress-free baking in the near future.

• **GALLON-SIZED SEALABLE FREEZER-SAFE BAGS.** These are found in local grocery stores. Preparing and placing many of these meals in freezer bags will allow for more room, and more meals, in the freezer.

• **DISPOSABLE FREEZER-SAFE BAKEWARE.** These are also found in local grocery stores. Having disposable bakeware will save your dishes from cracking, and in extreme cases, exploding. You'll also be able to prepare the meal and have an easy cleanup after baking.

• **PLASTIC WRAP AND ALUMINUM FOIL.** These will allow for extra sealing, protecting the food in the freezer and preventing the food from being burned when baking the meal.

Chicken

Crock-Pot White Chicken Chili

INGREDIENTS

2 (15.5-oz.) cans great northern beans, rinsed and drained

1 (8-oz.) can chopped mild green chilies

2 (15.25-oz.) cans corn

4 tsp. chicken bouillon granules

1 Tbsp. extra-virgin olive oil

1 small yellow onion, chopped

2 garlic cloves, minced

2 tsp. ground cumin

1 tsp. ground oregano

¼ tsp. ground cloves

¼ tsp. black pepper

¼ tsp. crushed red pepper flakes

1 boneless skinless chicken breast

4 cups water

FOR A NON-FREEZER MEAL: Place ingredients in a Crock-Pot. Add chicken and water last. Cook on low for 6–8 hours, or until chicken is cooked through. Shred chicken and serve.

TO FREEZE: Write expiration date, baking instructions, and name of the recipe on a gallon-sized plastic freezer bag. (Use 2 freezer bags if you decide to double the recipe for extra meals.) Add chicken to the bag first so it will be on top when cooking time arrives. Add remaining ingredients to the bag, except water. Seal the bag, removing as much air as possible, and then lay the bag flat in the freezer for optimal space. This meal can be safely frozen for up to 3 months.

FOR A FREEZER MEAL: The night prior to cooking, remove the meal from the freezer and allow to thaw in the refrigerator. After ingredients have thawed, pour the contents of the freezer bag into your Crock-Pot (with the chicken on top) and add the 4 cups of water. Cook on low for 6–8 hours, or until chicken is cooked through. Shred chicken and serve.

Chicken Sausage Broccoli Pockets

This meal is a family favorite for its simplicity. The meal is perfect as a quick grab-and-go for a rushed dinner.

INGREDIENTS

1 (12-oz.) package fully cooked chicken sausage links, thinly sliced

1 pound broccoli, cut into small florets and steamed

1 red bell pepper, cut into ¾-inch pieces

2 cloves garlic, minced

2 Tbsp. olive oil

½ tsp. salt

¼ tsp. black pepper

2 cups provolone cheese, grated

1½ pounds pizza dough

FOR A NON-FREEZER MEAL: Heat oven to 425 degrees. In a large bowl, mix together cooked sausage, cooked broccoli, bell pepper, garlic, and oil with kosher salt and black pepper. Add provolone and mix with the other ingredients.

Divide pizza dough into 8 pieces. On a lightly floured surface, roll each piece into a circle, about 6–7 inches in diameter. Spoon broccoli mixture onto one side of each round, leaving a ½-inch border. Fold dough over to form a semicircle and press firmly on the edges to seal. (Use water for added seal if needed.)

Place the pockets on a baking sheet lined with parchment paper. Transfer to the oven and cook the pockets for 20–25 minutes, or until golden brown. Serve with a side of your choosing.

TO FREEZE: Write expiration date, baking instructions, and name of the recipe on a gallon-sized plastic freezer bag. Prepare this recipe as directed, but do not bake in the oven. Place unbaked pockets on a baking sheet and place them in the freezer. After four hours, remove pockets from the freezer and wrap them in plastic wrap. Transfer pockets into the freezer bag. This meal can be safely frozen for up to 3 months.

FOR A FREEZER MEAL: The night prior to cooking, remove the meal from the freezer, remove plastic wrap, and allow to thaw in the refrigerator on a baking sheet. Preheat oven to 425 degrees. Cook for 15–20 minutes, or until golden brown.

IN A PINCH? Preheat oven to 425 degrees. Remove frozen pockets from the freezer, remove plastic wrap, and place them on a parchment-lined baking sheet. Cook the frozen pockets for 25–30 minutes, or until golden brown.

Chicken Tetrazzini

INGREDIENTS

6 Tbsp. butter

1 pound white mushrooms, sliced 1 inch thick

salt and pepper to taste

½ cup flour

3 cups milk

1 (14.5-oz.) can reduced-sodium chicken broth

3 cups grated Parmesan cheese

½ tsp. dried thyme leaves

1 pound linguine, broken in half or thirds (depending on personal preference)

1 rotisserie chicken, with skin removed and meat shredded (about 4 cups)

1 (10-oz.) bag of frozen peas, thawed and drained

FOR A NON-FREEZER MEAL: Preheat oven to 400 degrees. Bring a large pot of salted water to a boil to cook the pasta. In a large saucepan, melt 2 tablespoons of butter over high heat. Add mushrooms and season with salt and pepper. Cook until tender and browned, about 8–10 minutes. Transfer to a bowl and set aside.

In the same saucepan, melt remaining 4 tablespoons of butter over medium heat. Add flour, whisking for 1 minute. Gradually add milk and broth into flour and butter mixture. Bring to a boil, reduce to a simmer, and add 2 cups of Parmesan cheese and thyme. Season with salt and pepper.

Cook pasta 2 minutes less than package instructions. Drain and return to the pot. Add sauce, chicken, peas, and mushrooms. Mix well to combine. Place the prepared meal into a casserole-sized cookware and sprinkle with remaining Parmesan cheese. Bake for 25–30 minutes, or until browned. Let stand for 10 minutes before serving.

TO FREEZE: Write expiration date, baking instructions, and name of the recipe on a sheet of aluminum foil. Prepare the meal as directed, but do not bake. Place the pasta mixture in a disposable casserole-sized cookware and sprinkle with Parmesan cheese. Allow the meal to cool to room temperature. Cover tightly and seal with aluminum foil. This meal can be safely frozen for up to 3 months.

FOR A FREEZER MEAL: The night prior to cooking, remove the meal from the freezer and allow to thaw in the refrigerator. After ingredients have thawed, remove the old layer of aluminum foil and replace with a new layer. Bake at 400 degrees for 30 minutes, or until the center is warm. Remove the foil and bake until top is browned, an additional 20 minutes.

Chicken Enchiladas

This meal is a family staple in our home. It's simple but can be decorated with a variety and assortment of toppings to make each meal unique.

INGREDIENTS

2 boneless skinless chicken breasts, cooked and shredded

2 cups shredded pepper jack cheese

½ cup sour cream

1 (4.5-oz.) can chopped green chilies, drained

¼ cup chopped fresh cilantro (add more if desired)

8 soft taco flour tortillas

vegetable cooking spray

1 (8-oz.) bottle green taco sauce

1 (8-oz.) container sour cream

toppings: chopped tomatoes, chopped avocado, sliced green onions, sliced black olives, etc. as desired

FOR A NON-FREEZER MEAL: Preheat oven to 350 degrees. Stir first 5 ingredients together in a large bowl. Spoon ½ cup chicken mixture down the center of each tortilla. Roll each tortilla up.

Placed rolled tortillas, seam side down, in a lightly greased 9 × 13 baking dish.

Bake at 350 degrees for 30–35 minutes, or until golden brown. Stir together taco sauce and sour cream. Spoon over cooked enchiladas and sprinkle with desired toppings.

TO FREEZE: Write expiration date, baking instructions, and name of the recipe on a sheet of aluminum foil. Prepare the recipe as directed, but do not bake. Do not spread the taco sauce and sour cream on the enchiladas. Place the enchiladas in a disposable casserole-sized cookware. Cover with aluminum foil. Place in the freezer. This meal can be safely frozen for up to 1 month.

FOR A FREEZER MEAL: The night prior to cooking, remove meal from the freezer and allow to thaw in the refrigerator. Once the meal has thawed, bake at 350 degrees for 30–35 minutes, or until golden brown. Stir together taco sauce and sour cream. Spoon over cooked enchiladas and sprinkle with desired toppings. Enjoy.

IN A PINCH? Do not take the enchiladas out of the freezer until you're ready to bake the meal (bake frozen). Preheat oven to 350 degrees. Remove foil from the baking dish. Place a new sheet of foil over the frozen enchiladas. Bake for 30 minutes. Uncover and bake for another 15–20 minutes. Let cool for 10 minutes before serving.

Chicken Pesto Alfredo

INGREDIENTS

¼ cup butter

¼ cup flour

2 cups chicken broth

1 (16-oz.) box penne pasta (or other small pasta)

3–4 boneless skinless chicken breasts, cooked and cubed or shredded

4 cups shredded Italian cheese blend

3 cups fresh baby spinach, chopped

1 (14.5-oz.) can crushed tomatoes

1½ cups milk

3 Tbsp. basil pesto

¾ cup chopped crispy bacon

½ cup Italian seasoned breadcrumbs

½ cup shredded Parmesan cheese

1 Tbsp. extra-virgin olive oil

FOR A NON-FREEZER MEAL: Preheat oven to 350 degrees. Begin by making a white sauce: melt butter in a pan over medium heat. Sprinkle in flour over the melted butter and whisk constantly for 3–4 minutes. Add in chicken broth and whisk together. Cook over medium heat until the sauce is thick and bubbles up. Set the white sauce aside.

Cook the pasta according to package directions. Drain the noodles and place them in a large mixing bowl. Add in white sauce, cooked chicken, cheese, spinach, crushed tomatoes, milk, pesto, and ½ cup bacon. Mix well.

Pour pasta mixture into a prepared 9 × 13 baking dish.

In a separate bowl, mix together Parmesan cheese, breadcrumbs, remaining bacon, and olive oil.

Cover pasta with breadcrumb mixture and bake at 350 degrees for 45 minutes.

TO FREEZE: Write expiration date, baking instructions, and name of the recipe on a sheet of aluminum foil. Prepare the recipe as directed, but do not bake in the oven. Place meal in a disposable casserole-sized cookware, sealing properly with aluminum foil. Place in freezer. This meal can be safely frozen for up to 3 months.

FOR A FREEZER MEAL: The night prior to cooking, remove the meal from the freezer and allow it to thaw in the refrigerator. After ingredients have thawed, preheat the oven to 350 degrees. Remove the original aluminum foil covering and bake for 45 minutes, or until the center is warm. Enjoy.

Chicken Potpie

This meal is easy to put together for those busy nights that sneak up on each of us.

INGREDIENTS

2 top and bottom piece piecrusts

2–3 boneless skinless chicken breasts, cooked and shredded or cubed

1 (16-oz.) bag frozen hashbrowns

1 (6-oz.) bag frozen peas

1 (6-oz.) bag frozen carrots

¼ cup finely diced onion

2 (10.5-oz.) jars chicken or turkey gravy

salt and pepper to taste

FOR A NON-FREEZER MEAL: Preheat oven to 350 degrees. Thaw piecrusts and set aside. Mix shredded chicken, hash browns, peas, carrots, onion, and gravy in a large bowl. Add salt and pepper to taste.

When piecrusts have thawed, add potpie ingredients to piecrust. Place top crust on the pie and pinch the two crusts together at the seams. Poke a few holes on top of pie with a fork or knife.

Place potpie in the oven and cook for 35–45 minutes, or until top is golden brown.

TO FREEZE: Write expiration date, baking instructions, and name of the recipe on a sheet of aluminum foil. Prepare recipe according to directions, but do not bake. Place meal in a disposable casserole-sized pie tin cookware. Cover and seal with aluminum foil. Place in freezer. This meal can be safely frozen for up to 3 months.

FOR A FREEZER MEAL: The night prior to cooking, remove the meal from the freezer and allow to thaw in the refrigerator. After meal has thawed, cook as directed at 350 degrees for 35–45 minutes, or until center is warm.

Red Pepper Chicken

INGREDIENTS

1-2 boneless skinless chicken breast	1 small onion, diced
1 red bell pepper, sliced	1 tsp. crushed red pepper flakes
¼ cup extra virgin olive oil	½ tsp. black pepper
4 large garlic cloves, minced	¼ tsp. salt

FOR A NON-FREEZER MEAL: Place ingredients in Crock-Pot, adding chicken last. Cook on low for 6–8 hours, or until chicken is cooked through.

Serve with your choice of sides (rice, potatoes, salad, and so on).

TO FREEZE: Write expiration date, baking instructions, and name of recipe on a gallon-sized plastic freezer bag. (Use two freezer bags if you decide to double the recipe for extra meals.) Place all ingredients in the bag. Seal the bag, removing as much air as possible, and then lay bag flat in the freezer for optimal space. This meal can be safely frozen for up to 3 months.

FOR A FREEZER MEAL: The night prior to cooking, remove meal from freezer and allow to thaw in the refrigerator. After ingredients have thawed, pour the contents of freezer bag into your Crock-Pot. Cook on low for 6–8 hours or until chicken is cooked through. Serve with your choice of sides.

Cheesy Chicken Casserole

INGREDIENTS

2-3 boneless skinless chicken breasts, diced and uncooked

1 (10-oz.) can cream of mushroom or cream of chicken soup

2 cups shredded cheddar cheese

1 (6-oz.) box stuffing mix

⅓ cup water

4 Tbsp. butter, melted

FOR A NON-FREEZER MEAL: Preheat oven to 350 degrees. Grease a 9 × 13 baking dish with cooking spray. Spread diced chicken over the bottom of the pan. Top chicken with cream soup (mushroom or chicken) evenly. Sprinkle cheese evenly over casserole.

In a separate bowl, mix stuffing, water, and butter. Spread over top of the casserole. Bake uncovered for 40–45 minutes, or until chicken is cooked.

TO FREEZE: Write expiration date, baking instructions, and name of the recipe on a sheet of aluminum foil. Prepare recipe as directed, but do not bake. Place meal in a disposable casserole-sized cookware, covering and sealing with aluminum foil. Place in freezer. This meal can be safely frozen for up to 1 month.

FOR A FREEZER MEAL: The night prior to cooking, remove meal from the freezer and allow to thaw in the refrigerator. After ingredients have thawed, bake meal at 350 degrees for 40–45 minutes. Cover with aluminum foil if the top gets too brown in the oven before the casserole is cooked completely.

Lemon Pepper Chicken

INGREDIENTS

1–2 boneless skinless chicken breasts, uncooked

¼ cup extra virgin olive oil

1 lemon, juiced (about 3 tablespoons)

½ tsp. black pepper

¼ tsp. salt

FOR A NON-FREEZER MEAL: Place ingredients in a Crock-Pot, adding chicken last. Cook on low for 6–8 hours, or until chicken is cooked through.

Serve with your choice of side (salad, potatoes, rice, etc.).

TO FREEZE: Write expiration date, baking instructions, and name of the recipe on a gallon-sized plastic freezer bag. (Use two freezer bags if you decide to double the recipe for extra meals.) Place all ingredients in the bag. Seal bag, removing as much air as possible. Lay bag flat in the freezer for optimal space. This meal can be safely frozen for up to 3 months.

FOR A FREEZER MEAL: The night prior to cooking, remove meal from the freezer and allow to thaw in the refrigerator. After ingredients have thawed, pour the contents into your Crock-Pot. Cook on low for 6–8 hours, or until chicken is cooked through. Serve with your choice of side.

Fajitas

INGREDIENTS

1 pound boneless skinless chicken breasts or top sirloin steaks

2 Tbsp. olive oil

1 Tbsp. lime juice

1 garlic clove, minced

½ tsp. chili powder

½ tsp. ground cumin

½ tsp. crushed red pepper flakes

½ tsp. black pepper

½ tsp. salt

1 onion, chopped

2 small sweet peppers (green, red, or yellow)

8 flour tortillas

toppings: salsa, sour cream, shredded cheese, chopped tomatoes

FOR A NON-FREEZER MEAL: Slice chicken or steak into thin strips. In a large bowl, mix together 1 tablespoon olive oil, lime juice, garlic, chili powder, cumin, hot pepper flakes, black pepper, and salt. Add steak or chicken to coat; set aside.

Cut onion in half and slice into strips. Cut peppers into strips. In a large nonstick skillet over medium heat, heat remaining tablespoon of olive oil. Add onions and peppers, stirring for 3–4 minutes, until softened. Transfer to a bowl and set aside.

Add chicken or steak to the skillet and cook, stirring for about 5 minutes. Return onions and peppers to skillet and stir for about 1 minute.

To serve, spoon a portion of the meat mixture down the center of each tortilla, top with your desired toppings, and fold together.

TO FREEZE: Write expiration date, baking instructions, and name of the recipe on a gallon-sized plastic freezer bag. Cook meal as directed and place all the ingredients in freezer bag once the meal has cooled to room temperature. Do not freeze the toppings with the meal. This meal can be safely frozen for up to 1 month.

FOR A FREEZER MEAL: Remove meal from freezer and place in the refrigerator to thaw the night prior to cooking. After ingredients have thawed, reheat the meal either on the stove over low-medium heat, stirring frequently, or in the microwave. Eat and enjoy with your choice of toppings.

Orange Ginger Chicken

INGREDIENTS

1-2 boneless skinless chicken breasts, uncooked

2 oranges, juiced (about 1/3 cup of juice)

3 Tbsp. fresh ginger root, peeled and minced

2 Tbsp. honey

2 Tbsp. coconut oil

1 tsp. crushed red pepper flakes

FOR A NON-FREEZER MEAL: Place ingredients in a Crock-Pot, adding the chicken last. Cook on low for 6–8 hours, or until chicken is cooked through.

TO FREEZE: Write expiration date, baking instructions, and name of the recipe on a gallon-sized plastic freezer bag (use two freezer bags if you decide to double the recipe for extra meals). Place all ingredients in bag. Seal bag, removing as much air as possible, and then lay the bag flat in the freezer for optimal space. This meal can be safely frozen for up to 3 months.

FOR A FREEZER MEAL: The night prior to cooking, remove meal from freezer and allow to thaw in the refrigerator. After ingredients have thawed, pour the contents of the freezer bag into your Crock-Pot. Cook on low for 6–8 hours, or until the chicken is cooked through.

Chipotle Chicken Chili

This meal is a family favorite, and it is always served with a side of corn bread in our home. For an extra-spicy chili, add more chipotle peppers and chili powder to taste.

INGREDIENTS

2 Tbsp. olive oil

1 onion, diced

4 cloves garlic, minced

2 boneless skinless chicken breasts, diced

2 cups water

1 (14.5-oz.) can diced tomatoes

3 chipotle peppers in adobo sauce, minced

1 (15-oz.) can pinto beans, drained and rinsed

1 (15-oz.) can black beans, drained and rinsed

1 (15-oz.) can kidney beans, drained and rinsed

1 Tbsp. chili powder

1 Tbsp. ground cumin

1 tsp. salt

¼ cup masa harina

1 lime, juiced

Toppings: sour cream, grated sharp cheddar cheese, cilantro, lime wedges

FOR A NON-FREEZER MEAL: Heat olive oil in a large pot over medium heat, and then add onions and garlic. Cook until onions soften, about 3 minutes. Add chicken and cook until lightly browned. Add water.

Add tomatoes, chipotle peppers, beans, chili powder, cumin, and salt. Stir to combine. Cover pot and cook for 1 hour. Add masa harina and lime juice to chili. Stir and cook for 10 more minutes. Serve with your choice of toppings.

TO FREEZE: Write expiration date, baking instructions, and name of the recipe on a gallon-sized plastic freezer bag. Prepare meal according to the directions. Allow cooked meal to cool before placing into freezer bag. Do not freeze the toppings. This meal can be safely frozen for up to 2 months.

FOR A FREEZER MEAL: The night prior to cooking, remove meal from freezer and allow to thaw in the refrigerator. After ingredients have thawed, pour contents of freezer bag into a large cooking pan. Warm the contents of the meal over low-medium heat. Once contents have re-warmed, eat and enjoy with your choice of toppings.

Chicken Cordon Bleu Casserole

INGREDIENTS

½ cup milk	½ cup cubed swiss cheese
1 egg	½ cup diced ham
2–3 boneless skinless chicken breasts, cubed	1 (10.75-oz.) can cream of chicken soup
dry breadcrumbs	1 cup milk

FOR A NON-FREEZER MEAL: Preheat oven to 350 degrees. Mix milk and egg together. Dip chicken in egg-milk mixture and toss with breadcrumbs, coating well. Cook chicken until golden. Place chicken in a baking dish, and then add cheese and ham. Mix cream of chicken soup with 1 cup of milk and pour over casserole. Bake for 30–35 minutes.

TO FREEZE: Write expiration date, baking instructions, and name of the recipe on a sheet of aluminum foil. Prepare recipe without adding 1 cup of milk and cream of chicken soup to the meal. Do not bake. Place meal in a disposable casserole-sized cookware. Cover and seal tightly with aluminum foil. Place in freezer. This meal can be safely frozen for up to 3 months.

FOR A FREEZER MEAL: The night prior to cooking, remove meal from freezer and allow to thaw in the refrigerator. After ingredients have thawed, mix 1 cup milk mixture and cream of chicken soup and add to casserole. Bake for 30–35 minutes at 350 degrees, or until the center is warm.

Chicken Divan

INGREDIENTS

7 cups uncooked rice

1-2 boneless skinless chicken breasts, cubed

8 cups chopped broccoli florets

4 cups mayonnaise

2 cups sour cream

4 cups shredded cheddar cheese

1 Tbsp. garlic powder

1 Tbsp. onion powder

salt and pepper to taste

FOR A NON-FREEZER MEAL: Preheat oven to 350 degrees. Cook rice according to labeled directions, and set aside when done. Cook cubed chicken until golden and no longer pink. Once cooked, set chicken aside. Steam broccoli, cut into bite sized pieces, set aside once cooked.

Place rice, chicken, and broccoli into a bowl and mix with the remaining ingredients except 1 cup of cheese. Use the 1 cup of cheese to sprinkle on top of the meal after it's been mixed and place into a 9 × 13 baking dish.

Cook meal for 25–35 minutes, or until the middle is done.

TO FREEZE: Write expiration date, baking instructions, and name of the recipe on a sheet of aluminum foil. Prepare recipe as directed but do not bake. Place meal in a disposable casserole-sized cookware. Allow meal to cool to room temperature. Tightly seal and cover with aluminum foil and place meal in freezer. This meal can be safely frozen for up to 3 months.

FOR A FREEZER MEAL: The night prior to cooking, remove meal from freezer and allow to thaw in the refrigerator. After ingredients have thawed, bake as directed at 350 degrees for 25–35 minutes, or until the center is warm.

Crock-Pot Chicken Dumplings

Chicken dumpling meals are a personal favorite. They always make a great comfort food.

INGREDIENTS

3 boneless skinless chicken breasts

1 onion, chopped

2 cups frozen mixed vegetables

2 (10.5-oz.) cans cream of chicken soup

1 can refrigerated biscuits

FOR A NON-FREEZER MEAL: Combine all ingredients except biscuits in a Crock-Pot. Cook on low for 6–8 hours or high for 4–5 hours. An hour before serving, shred chicken with two large forks. Drop in biscuit dough. Cover and cook for another hour. The biscuits are done when you can insert a knife into them and it comes out clean.

TO FREEZE: Write expiration date, baking instructions, and name of the recipe on a gallon-sized plastic freezer bag. Place chicken, onion, mixed vegetables, and cream of chicken soup in the bag. Set can of refrigerated biscuits aside for the day of cooking. Place in freezer. This meal can be safely frozen for up to 3 months.

FOR A FREEZER MEAL: The night prior to cooking, remove meal from freezer and allow to thaw in the refrigerator. After ingredients have thawed, place in a Crock-Pot. Cover and cook on low for 6–8 hours, stirring periodically. Add refrigerated biscuits an hour prior to serving.

Stovetop Chicken Dumplings

INGREDIENTS

For Soup

3 boneless skinless chicken breasts, cubed

1 cup chopped yellow onion

1 cup sliced celery

¼ cup flour

2 cups sliced carrots

½ tsp. ground thyme

10 cups chicken broth

For Dumplings

2 cups flour

1 Tbsp. baking powder

¾ cup buttermilk

FOR A NON-FREEZER MEAL: In a large pot, cook chicken and onions over medium heat until chicken is browned, about 6–8 minutes. Add celery and cook for another 2–3 minutes, stirring occasionally.

Add ¼ cup flour, and slowly add carrots, thyme, and chicken broth, stirring well. Bring mixture to a boil, cover, and reduce heat. Simmer for 20 minutes, stirring occasionally.

While simmering, prepare dumplings by mixing flour and baking powder. Slowly add buttermilk, stirring well to combine.

After simmering, drop tablespoon-sized dough balls into chicken stew. Cover again and finish cooking over medium-low heat for 15 minutes, or until dumplings are fully cooked.

TO FREEZE: Write expiration date, baking instructions, and name of the recipe on a gallon-sized plastic freezer bag. Prepare recipe as directed and allow meal to cool to room temperature before storing in bags. Remove as much air as possible from the bag before placing in the freezer. This meal can be safely frozen for up to 4 months.

FOR A FREEZER MEAL: The night prior to cooking, remove meal from freezer and allow to thaw in the refrigerator. After ingredients have thawed, reheat the meal on the stovetop over low-medium heat, or warm in the microwave. Enjoy.

Chicken and Wild Rice

INGREDIENTS

1 (6.2-oz.) box wild rice with seasoning packet

1 (10.5-oz.) can cream of mushroom soup

1 (10.5-oz.) can cream of chicken soup

1½ cups of water

1 small can mushrooms, drained and diced

6 boneless skinless chicken thighs, uncooked

1 cup slivered almonds

FOR A NON-FREEZER MEAL: Preheat oven to 350 degrees. Mix together uncooked rice with seasoning packet, both soups, and water. Stir in diced mushrooms. Pour into a casserole-sized cookware. Top with boneless skinless chicken thighs and sprinkle with slivered almonds.

Cook uncovered for 1 hour, or until chicken juices run clear and rice is tender.

TO FREEZE: Write expiration date, baking instructions, and name of the recipe on a sheet of aluminum foil. Prepare recipe as directed, but do not bake. Assemble meal in a disposable casserole-sized cookware. Cool to room temperature before placing in freezer. Cover and seal tightly with aluminum foil. Place in freezer. This meal can be safely frozen for up to 4 months.

FOR A FREEZER MEAL: The night prior to cooking, remove meal from freezer and allow to thaw in the refrigerator. After ingredients have thawed, cook as directed for 1 hour at 350 degrees.

Chicken and Green Chili

INGREDIENTS

1 small yellow onion, diced

½ pound mushrooms, sliced

¼ cup butter

1 (10.5-oz.) can cream of mushroom soup

1 (10.5-oz.) can cream of chicken soup

1 (14.5-oz.) can diced tomatoes, undrained

1 (4-oz.) can diced green chilies

1 tsp. garlic powder

2 Tbsp. chili powder

1 Tbsp. chicken broth

12 soft corn tortillas, torn in fourths

2–3 boneless skinless chicken breasts, cooked and cubed

4 cups shredded cheddar cheese

FOR A NON-FREEZER MEAL: Preheat oven to 350 degrees. In a large skillet, cook onion and mushrooms in butter over medium heat. Add cream soups, tomatoes, chilies, seasonings, and broth. Line a baking dish with half of the tortilla pieces. Spread half of the chopped chicken over the tortillas and top with half the sauce, then half the cheese. Repeat the layers. Cook for 30 minutes and enjoy.

TO FREEZE: Write expiration date, baking instructions, and name of the recipe on a sheet of aluminum foil. Prepare recipe as directed, but do not bake. Assemble meal in a disposable casserole-sized cookware. Cool to room temperature before placing in the freezer. Cover and seal tightly with a sheet of aluminum foil. Place in freezer. This meal can be safely frozen for up to 4 months.

FOR A FREEZER MEAL: The night prior to cooking, remove meal from freezer and allow to thaw in the refrigerator. After ingredients have thawed, bake according to the directions. Cook meal at 350 degrees for 30 minutes, or until the center is heated through. Cover with aluminum foil if cooking time is needed for longer than 30 minutes (to prevent the top from browning).

Beef

Quesadilla Casserole

INGREDIENTS

1 pound lean ground beef

½ cup diced onion

1 (16-oz.) can tomato sauce

1 (15-oz.) can black beans, drained and rinsed

1 (15.25-oz.) can corn, undrained

1 (4-oz.) can green chilies, undrained

2 tsp. chili powder

1 tsp. ground cumin

1 tsp. dried minced garlic

½ tsp. oregano

½ tsp. crushed red pepper

6 flour tortillas

2 cups shredded cheddar cheese

FOR A NON-FREEZER MEAL: Preheat oven to 350 degrees. Brown beef and onion in a large skillet over medium-high heat. Add tomato sauce, beans, corn, and green chilies. Mix well. Stir in all spices except the red pepper. Bring to a boil, reduce heat to low, and simmer for 5 minutes. Add red pepper to taste if desired.

Spread a third of beef mixture onto the bottom of a casserole-sized dish. Top with 3 tortillas, overlapping as needed. Layer a third of beef mixture and ½ cup of shredded cheese. Repeat with remaining tortillas, beef, and cheese. Cook in the oven for 15–20 minutes.

TO FREEZE: Write expiration date, baking instructions, and name of the recipe on a sheet of aluminum foil. Prepare recipe as directed but do not bake. Assemble meal in a disposable casserole-sized cookware. Allow meal to cool to room temperature before storing in freezer. Cover and seal tightly with aluminum foil. Place in freezer. This meal can be safely frozen for up to 3 months.

FOR A FREEZER MEAL: The night prior to cooking, remove meal from freezer and allow to thaw in the refrigerator. After ingredients have thawed, bake in the oven as directed at 350 degrees for 15–20 minutes.

Crock-Pot Hamburger and Veggie Soup

INGREDIENTS

1 pound lean ground beef, cooked

4 carrots, peeled and sliced

2 small potatoes, peeled and cut into 1-inch chunks

1 small onion, diced

2 (14.5-oz.) cans diced tomatoes

1 Tbsp. extra-virgin olive oil

2 garlic cloves, minced

1 Tbsp. Italian seasoning

¼ tsp. pepper

4 tsp. beef bouillon granules

4 cups water

FOR A NON-FREEZER MEAL: Cook ground beef over medium heat on stove. Drain excess fat and place beef in Crock-Pot. Combine remaining ingredients together in Crock-Pot, adding water in last. Cook on low for 6–8 hours.

TO FREEZE: Write expiration date, baking instructions, and name of the recipe on a gallon-sized plastic freezer bag. Cook ground beef. Allow beef to cool to room temperature before placing in freezer bag. Add remaining ingredients (except water) into freezer bag. To keep potatoes from browning, chop them last and add them to your freezer bag. Remove as much air from freezer bag as possible, seal, and lay flat in your freezer. This meal can be safely frozen for up to 3 months.

FOR A FREEZER MEAL: The night prior to cooking, remove meal from freezer and allow to thaw in the refrigerator. After ingredients have thawed, pour contents of freezer bag into your Crock-Pot and add water. Cook on low for 6–8 hours.

Tamale Pie

INGREDIENTS

Filling

3 Tbsp. olive oil

2 pounds lean ground beef or turkey

1 large onion, chopped

2 jalapeño chilies, minced

1 Tbsp. ground cumin

2 tsp. coarse salt

¼ tsp. ground pepper

1 (14.5-oz.) can crushed tomatoes

2 (15.25-oz.) cans corn, rinsed and drained

Cornmeal Crust

1½ cups yellow cornmeal

1½ cups water, cold

2½ cups water (to boil)

coarse salt to taste

ground pepper to taste

4 Tbsp. butter

shredded cheese to top

FOR A NON-FREEZER MEAL: Preheat oven to 375 degrees and begin to make filling. Heat 2 tablespoons of oil in a large skillet over medium-high heat. Brown ground beef or turkey, stirring occasionally. When completely cooked, drain excess oil and transfer meat to a bowl.

Reduce heat to medium temperature and add remaining tablespoon of oil. Cook onion, jalapeño, and cumin until soft, about five minutes, stirring occasionally. Season with salt and pepper. Return meat to pan. Add tomatoes and corn. Stir until combined.

To make cornmeal crust, mix cornmeal with cold water. In a medium saucepan, bring 2½ cups water, salt, and pepper to a boil. Gradually stir in cornmeal mixture. Reduce heat to low and stir often until very thick, about 4–5 minutes. Remove from heat and stir in butter until melted.

Pour crust into two 9-inch pie tins. Once pies are prepared, pour meat mixture into the pie tins and sprinkle with cheese. Cook for 45–60 minutes on a rimmed baking sheet until filling is bubbly and cheese is melted.

TO FREEZE: Write expiration date, baking instructions, and name of the recipe on a sheet of aluminum foil. Prepare meal as directed, using disposable pie tins, but do not bake. Do not add cheese on top as directed. Let the pies cool completely before placing in the freezer. Cover and seal with aluminum foil. Place in freezer. This meal can be safely frozen for up to 4 months.

FOR A FREEZER MEAL: The night prior to cooking, remove meal from freezer and allow to thaw in the refrigerator. After ingredients have thawed, sprinkle the top with cheese and bake on a rimmed baking sheet as directed, uncovered, at 375 degrees for 45–60 minutes.

Meatloaf and Chili Sauce

This is one of the many meals in this cookbook that our little ones eat willingly. We serve this meal with a side of vegetables and garlic bread.

INGREDIENTS

½ cup milk	¾ cup chili sauce
4 slices sandwich bread	1 cup fresh parsley
1½ pounds ground sirloin	½ cup grated Parmesan cheese
1½ pounds ground pork	2 large eggs
2 small onions, chopped	1½ tsp. salt
6 cloves garlic, minced	½ tsp. pepper

FOR A NON-FREEZER MEAL: Preheat oven to 350 degrees. In a large bowl, slowly pour milk over bread and let it soak for about 30 seconds. Add sirloin, pork, onion, garlic, ½ cup chili sauce, parsley, Parmesan cheese, eggs, salt, and pepper. Mix until combined.

Divide mixture in half and gently pat each into a log. Place each in a loaf pan but do not press down or into the corners. Bake for 50 minutes. Pull out of the oven and brush the tops with the remaining chili sauce. Continue cooking until juices run clear, an additional 10–15 minutes. Remove from oven and let cool.

TO FREEZE: Write expiration date, baking instructions, and name of the recipe on a sheet of aluminum foil. Prepare and cook meal as directed using a disposable casserole-sized cookware. Allow the dish to cool completely to room temperature before placing in the freezer. Cover and seal tightly with aluminum foil. Place in freezer. This meal can be safely frozen for up to 2 months.

FOR A FREEZER MEAL: The night prior to cooking, remove meal from freezer and allow to thaw in the refrigerator. After ingredients have thawed, reheat in the oven at 300 degrees for 15 minutes, or until the center is warm.

Sloppy Joes

INGREDIENTS

3 tsp. olive oil

1 pound lean ground beef

2 tsp. steak seasoning (or sloppy joe seasoning)

2 Tbsp. brown sugar

½ onion, finely chopped

1 carrot, grated

1 red pepper, diced

2 garlic cloves, minced

1 Tbsp. red wine vinegar

1 Tbsp. Worcestershire sauce

2 (8-oz.) cans tomato sauce

2 Tbsp. tomato paste

1 Tbsp. maple syrup

salt to taste

FOR A NON-FREEZER MEAL: Add 1 teaspoon of olive oil and ground beef to a large skillet. Cook beef until no pink remains, over medium-high heat. Drain excess fat. In a separate bowl, combine steak seasoning and brown sugar. Mix this with cooked ground beef.

In another pan add remaining 2 teaspoons of olive oil. Add carrot, onion, red pepper, garlic, red wine vinegar, and Worcestershire sauce. Cook until veggies are tender, about 4–5 minutes.

Add cooked meat, tomato sauce, tomato paste, and maple syrup to the pan. Stir to combine. Reduce heat to simmer and cook for an additional 5 minutes. Season the mixture with salt as needed. To serve, place mixture between two hamburger buns and enjoy.

TO FREEZE: Write expiration date, baking instructions, and name of the recipe on a gallon-sized plastic freezer bag. Prepare and bake meal according to directions. Cool to room temperature. Place meal in a plastic freezer bag. Remove as much air as possible. Place in freezer. This meal can be safely frozen for up to 3 months.

FOR A FREEZER MEAL: The night prior to cooking, remove meal from freezer and allow to thaw in the refrigerator. After ingredients have thawed, warm mixture in a saucepan over low-medium heat until warmed through. Serve between two hamburger buns and enjoy.

Tex-Mex Beef Enchiladas

INGREDIENTS

Sauce

1½ Tbsp. olive oil

¼ cups all-purpose flour

1¾ cups reduced-sodium chicken broth

1½ Tbsp. chili powder

1 small chipotle chili in adobo sauce

1 Tbsp. adobo sauce

¾ cup water

Filling

½ Tbsp. olive oil

1 small onion, chopped

2 garlic cloves, minced

1 pound lean ground beef

salt and pepper to taste

Other

8 corn tortillas

1½ cups shredded cheddar cheese

¼ cup chopped cilantro

FOR A NON-FREEZER MEAL: To make sauce, heat 1½ tablespoons of oil over medium heat in a saucepan. Add flour and whisk occasionally, about 1 minute. Add broth, chili powder, chipotle, adobe sauce, and water. Bring to a boil, whisking continually. Reduce heat and simmer until lightly thickened, about 10 minutes.

To make filling: In a skillet, heat ½ tablespoon of oil over medium-high heat. Add onion, garlic, and beef. Season with salt and pepper, to taste. Cook for about 8–10 minutes, or until beef has no remaining pink.

Preheat oven to 350 degrees. Spoon ¼ cup of sauce in the bottom of a 9 × 13 baking dish.

Warm tortillas in the oven for about 10 minutes. Fill each tortilla with ¼ cup beef mixture and 2 tablespoons of cheese. Tightly roll up.

Place the enchiladas, seam side down, in a baking dish. Top with remaining sauce and sprinkle with cheese. Bake uncovered for 15–20 minutes, or until bubbly. Let cool for 10 minutes before serving. Sprinkle cilantro on baked enchiladas.

TO FREEZE: Write expiration date, baking instructions, and name of the recipe on a sheet of aluminum foil. Prepare meal according to directions, making the enchiladas and sauce. Arrange enchiladas in a disposable casserole-sized cookware, without sauce on top and bottom. Place sauce in a separate freezer-safe sealable bag. Seal bag and remove as much air as possible. Place both the sauce and tightly covered disposable casserole dish in freezer once the meal has cooled to room temperature. This meal can be safely frozen for up to 2 months.

FOR A FREEZER MEAL: The night prior to cooking, remove meal from freezer and allow to thaw in the refrigerator. Preheat oven to 350 degrees. Remove foil from the baking dish. Pour sauce on top and sprinkle with cheese. Place a new sheet of foil over thawed enchiladas. Bake for 30 minutes. Uncover and bake for another 15 minutes. Let cool for 10 minutes before serving.

IN A PINCH? Thaw sauce in the refrigerator overnight or thaw under running warm water. Do not take the enchiladas out of the freezer until you're ready to bake the meal (bake frozen). Preheat oven to 350 degrees. Remove foil from baking dish. Pour sauce on top and sprinkle with cheese. Place a new sheet of foil over frozen enchiladas. Bake for 30 minutes. Uncover and bake for another 15–20 minutes. Let cool for 10 minutes before serving.

Beefy Lasagna

We love our lasagna meals with a side of garlic bread!

INGREDIENTS

12 lasagna noodles	1 tsp. salt
1 (24-oz.) container small curd cottage cheese	2½ cups shredded mozzarella cheese, divided
1 (16-oz.) container ricotta cheese	1 pound lean ground beef
2 large eggs	½ cup chopped onion
½ cup pesto	2 (24-oz.) cans tomato pasta sauce

FOR A NON-FREEZER MEAL: Preheat oven to 375 degrees. Cook noodles according to package directions. Stir together cottage cheese, ricotta cheese, eggs, pesto, salt, and 1 cup of mozzarella cheese.

Cook ground beef and onion in a large skillet over medium heat. Stir often, until meat crumbles and is no longer pink. Drain the excess fat and stir in pasta sauce.

Layer 1 cup of beef mixture, 3 noodles, and 2½ cups of cottage cheese mixture in a lightly greased 9 × 13 baking dish. Top with 3 noodles, 2 cups of beef mixture, and 3 more noodles. Top with remaining cottage cheese mixture, 3 noodles, and beef mixture. Sprinkle with remaining 1½ cups mozzarella cheese.

Cover with aluminum foil and bake for 40–45 minutes. Uncover and bake for an additional 20 minutes. Let stand for 10–15 minutes to cool.

TO FREEZE: Write expiration date, baking instructions, and name of the recipe on a sheet of aluminum foil. Prepare meal according to directions but do not bake. Assemble meal in a disposable casserole-sized cookware. Allow meal to cool to room temperature before placing in the freezer. Cover and seal tightly with aluminum foil. Place in freezer. This meal can be safely frozen for up to 3 months.

FOR A FREEZER MEAL: The night prior to cooking, remove meal from freezer and allow to thaw in the refrigerator. After ingredients have thawed, remove current sheet of aluminum foil and replace with a fresh sheet of aluminum foil. Bake as directed at 375 degrees. Bake covered for 40–45 minutes, and then uncover and bake for an additional 15–20 minutes, or until the center is warmed.

Easy Lasagna

INGREDIENTS

½ cup chopped onion

2 garlic cloves, minced

1 pound ground beef

½ pound pork sausage

2 (28-oz.) cans spaghetti sauce

1 (14.5-oz.) can crushed Italian tomatoes

2 cups shredded mozzarella cheese

2 cups shredded Italian-blend cheese

12 lasagna noodles, cooked al dente

Parmesan cheese, grated

FOR A NON-FREEZER MEAL: Preheat oven to 375 degrees. In large skillet over medium heat, sauté onions. Add garlic and stir for 1 minute. Add beef and sausage. Cook until browned with no pink remaining. Drain excess fat, and stir in sauce and tomatoes.

Spread a thin layer of meat sauce onto bottom of a 9 × 13 baking dish. Arrange a layer of cooked lasagna noodles over the sauce. Sprinkle mozzarella cheese and Italian-blend cheese over the lasagna noodles. Repeat layers with the last layer being sauce.

Cover with aluminum foil and bake for 45–50 minutes. Take foil off and bake for another 15 minutes. Let cool for 10–15 minutes. Sprinkle Parmesan cheese on top before serving.

TO FREEZE: Write expiration date, baking instructions, and name of the recipe on a sheet of aluminum foil. Prepare dish according to directions, but do not bake in the oven. Assemble meal in a disposable casserole-sized cookware. Allow meal to cool to room temperature before placing in freezer. Cover and seal tightly with aluminum foil. Place in freezer. This meal can be safely frozen for up to 4 months.

FOR A FREEZER MEAL: The night prior to cooking, remove meal from freezer and allow to thaw in the refrigerator. After ingredients have thawed remove current layer of aluminum foil and replace with a fresh sheet. Heat the oven to 375 degrees and bake meal covered for 45–50 minutes. Then bake uncovered for an additional 15 minutes, or until center is warm. Set aside for 10 minutes, allowing meal to cool before serving. Sprinkle Parmesan cheese on top before serving. Enjoy.

Hamburger Patties

These patties are spicy due to the variety of spices in this recipe. If a milder hamburger patty is desired, replace the different spices with breadcrumbs.

INGREDIENTS

4 tsp. paprika

3 tsp. black pepper

2½ tsp. fine sea salt

1 tsp. dark brown sugar

1 tsp. garlic powder

1 tsp. onion powder

2 pounds lean ground beef

FOR A NON-FREEZER MEAL: Combine all spices into a bowl and mix together. In another bowl, add ground beef and about ¾ of spice mixture. Mix together well. Shape meat into hamburger patties and place on a baking sheet covered with parchment paper.

Sprinkle both sides of the hamburger with the leftover spice mixture. Cook burgers on grill or stovetop.

TO FREEZE: Write expiration date, baking instructions, and name of the recipe on a gallon-sized plastic freezer bag. Prepare meal according to directions, but do not cook. Shape meat into hamburger patties and place on a parchment-lined baking sheet. Place parchment paper in between layers of patties. Freeze for four hours. Remove patties from baking sheet and transfer to a gallon-sized freezer safe bag. Seal bag, removing as much air as possible. Place patties back in the freezer. This meal can be safely frozen for up to 3 months.

FOR A FREEZER MEAL: The night prior to cooking, remove patties from freezer and allow to thaw in the refrigerator. After patties have thawed, cook them on grill or stovetop.

Pizza Pockets

Making these pizza pockets with different toppings will create variety when eating. The more the variety, the more exciting eating the pockets will be when cooking time comes.

INGREDIENTS

Crust

3½ cups flour

1 tsp. sea salt

1 cup melted butter

1 cup plain yogurt

Pizza Sauce

1½ cups tomato sauce

½ tsp. garlic powder

1½ tsp. ground oregano

1½ tsp. ground basil

toppings: cheese, olives, pepperoni, green peppers, lean ground beef

FOR A NON-FREEZER MEAL: Preheat oven to 400 degrees. Begin by making the crust. Stir all crust ingredients together until thoroughly mixed. Make pizza sauce by stirring together sauce ingredients and simmering over a low-medium heat.

Roll out dough and create smaller circles using a large cup or circular cookie cutter. Roll out circle even more. Place 1–2 tablespoons of pizza sauce in the center, along with your choice of toppings.

Fold the dough in half using a fork to seal the edges together. Poke a few holes in the top of each pocket to allow steam to escape during baking.

Bake at 400 degrees for 20–25 minutes, or until golden brown.

TO FREEZE: Write expiration date, baking instructions, and name of the recipe on a gallon-sized plastic freezer bag. Prepare meal as directed but do not bake in the oven. Lay unbaked pizza pockets on a cookie sheet lined with parchment paper. Freeze for three hours. Take them off cookie sheet and wrap frozen pockets in plastic wrap. Put them into labeled freezer bag. Place pizza pockets back in freezer, removing as much air as possible. This meal can be safely frozen for up to 4 months.

FOR A FREEZER MEAL: The night prior to cooking, remove meal from freezer and allow to thaw in the refrigerator. Remove plastic wrap from pizza pockets and place on a baking sheet. After pockets have thawed, bake at 400 degrees for 20–25 minutes.

IN A PINCH? Bake pizza pockets frozen. Remove plastic wrap from frozen pizza pockets and place on a baking sheet. Preheat oven to 400 degrees and bake for 30–35 minutes, or until golden.

Pizza Stromboli

INGREDIENTS

pre-packaged pizza dough

½ cup pizza sauce

¾ cup chopped deli ham

¾ cup sliced mushrooms

½ cup chopped spinach

½ cup chopped red pepper

1 Tbsp. parsley, minced

garlic powder (to sprinkle on top)

Italian seasoning (to sprinkle on top)

1½ cup shredded Italian mix cheese

1½ cup shredded mozzarella cheese

additional desired toppings (ground beef, pepperoni, olives)

1 egg

1 Tbsp. water

FOR A NON-FREEZER MEAL: Preheat oven to 375 degrees. On a lightly floured surface, roll out the dough to make a large rectangle, about 10 × 14 inches. Spread pizza sauce, leaving a 1-inch border. Sprinkle the other items in order: ham, mushrooms, spinach, red pepper, parsley, garlic powder, Italian seasoning, and the cheeses. Sprinkle on additional toppings as desired.

Mix egg and water to make an egg wash. Using a pastry brush, paint the border of one long edge with egg wash. Starting at the opposite long end (the end without the egg wash), roll up dough into a cylinder, pinching the edges to seal.

Place on a baking sheet and brush the top of Stromboli with remaining egg wash. Bake for 25–30 minutes, or until golden brown. Let stand for 10 minutes before serving.

TO FREEZE: Write expiration date, baking instructions, and name of the recipe on a sheet of aluminum foil. Prepare recipe as directed, but do not bake. Lay uncooked pizza Stromboli on a cookie sheet lined with parchment paper. Freeze for 4 hours. Take Stromboli off cookie sheet and wrap with plastic wrap. Wrap a second time with sheet of aluminum foil. Return to freezer. This meal can be safely frozen for up to 4 months.

FOR A FREEZER MEAL: The night prior to cooking, remove Stromboli from freezer and allow to thaw in the refrigerator. After it has thawed, bake as directed at 375 degrees for 25–30 minutes or until the center is warm.

IN A PINCH? Heat oven to 375 degrees. Remove frozen Stromboli from freezer and place on a parchment-lined baking sheet. Bake at 375 degrees for 35–40 minutes, or until golden brown.

Meatballs

INGREDIENTS

1 medium carrot, grated	1 cup breadcrumbs
½ onion, finely chopped	3 Tbsp. ketchup
2 cloves garlic, minced	1¼ tsp. salt
⅓ cup parsley, minced	½ tsp. pepper
½ cup Parmesan cheese	1 pound lean ground beef
1 egg	

FOR A NON-FREEZER MEAL: Preheat oven to 400 degrees. Cover bottom of a 9 × 13 baking dish with aluminum foil. In a large bowl, combine carrot, onion, garlic, parsley, Parmesan, egg, breadcrumbs, ketchup, salt, and pepper. Mix in ground beef (use your hands to combine as needed).

Roll meat mixture into meatballs, about 2 tablespoons per meatball. Place in the casserole dish, leaving about an inch between each meatball. Bake for 18–20 minutes. Allow to cool for 5 minutes before serving.

TO FREEZE: Write expiration date, baking instructions, and name of the recipe on a gallon-sized plastic freezer bag. Bake meatballs according to the directions, and allow them to cool to room temperature. Place meatballs in the freezer bag. Remove as much air as possible. Place in freezer. This meal can be safely frozen for up to 4 months.

FOR A FREEZER MEAL: The night prior to cooking, remove meal from freezer and allow to thaw in the refrigerator. After meatballs have thawed, warm them in tomato sauce over low-medium heat, stirring frequently as to not burn the sauce.

Beef Stroganoff

INGREDIENTS

2–3 pounds stew meat, cubed	1½ cups beef broth
1 tsp. salt	1 Tbsp. ketchup
¼ tsp. black pepper	⅓ cup flour
1 medium yellow onion, diced	6 Tbsp. apple juice
¼ tsp. garlic salt	1 cup sliced mushrooms
1 Tbsp. Worcestershire sauce	½ cup sour cream

FOR A NON-FREEZER MEAL: Place cubed stew meat, salt, pepper, and onion in Crock-Pot. In a small bowl, combine garlic salt, Worcestershire sauce, beef broth, and ketchup. Pour over meat. Cook on high for 4–6 hours or low for 8–10 hours.

About 30 minutes before serving, combine flour and apple juice in a small bowl, and whisk together. Pour flour mixture into Crock-Pot, whisking frequently to avoid clumps. Add the mushrooms and stir. Cook on high for an additional 30 minutes. Stir in sour cream just before serving.

Serve over rice, pasta, or potatoes.

TO FREEZE: Write expiration date, baking instructions, and name of the recipe on a sheet of aluminum foil. Prepare and cook this meal as directed in a disposable casserole-sized cookware. Allow the meal to cool to room temperature. Cover and seal with aluminum foil. Place in the freezer. This meal can be safely frozen for up to 3 months.

FOR A FREEZER MEAL: The night prior to cooking, remove meal from freezer and allow to thaw in the refrigerator. After ingredients have thawed, warm over medium-low heat in a saucepan. Cook until heated through. Stir to prevent burning.

Goulash

INGREDIENTS

1 pound lean ground beef

1 tsp. garlic powder

1 tsp. onion powder

2 cups elbow macaroni

1 (15-oz.) can tomato soup

1 (6-oz.) can tomato paste

2 Tbsp. Italian seasoning

1 (15.25-oz.) can corn, drained

2 cups shredded cheese

FOR A NON-FREEZER MEAL: Preheat oven to 350 degrees. Brown ground beef with garlic powder and onion powder. Cook until no pink remains. Drain excess fat and set aside. Cook noodles al dente according to package instructions. Drain and set aside.

In a large bowl, combine tomato soup, tomato paste, Italian seasoning, noodles, and ground beef. Stir in corn. Transfer to an ungreased baking dish and top with your choice of shredded cheese.

Bake for 30–40 minutes, or until cheese is melted and bubbly.

TO FREEZE: Write expiration date, baking instructions, and name of the recipe on a sheet of aluminum foil. Prepare meal as directed but do not bake. Assemble meal in a disposable casserole-sized cookware. Allow meal to cool to room temperature. Cover and seal with aluminum foil. Place in freezer. This meal can be safely frozen for up to 4 months.

FOR A FREEZER MEAL: The night prior to cooking, remove meal from freezer and allow to thaw in the refrigerator. After ingredients have thawed, bake uncovered at 350 degrees for 30–40 minutes, or until the center is heated through.

Pasta

Mac and Cheese

INGREDIENTS

1 pound short pasta of your choice

6 Tbsp. unsalted butter

¼ cup flour

5 cups milk

¼ tsp. salt

¼ tsp. pepper

4 cups shredded cheddar cheese

1 cup Parmesan cheese

1 cup crushed buttery crackers

FOR A NON-FREEZER MEAL: Heat oven to 350 degrees. Cook pasta 2 minutes less than package directions recommend. Drain and return to the pot.

In a large pot, melt butter over medium heat. Add flour, whisking constantly. Gradually add in milk, salt, and pepper. Bring to a boil, reduce heat, and simmer, whisking occasionally, until the sauce thickens slightly, about 10–15 minutes. Remove from heat and gradually stir in cheddar cheese and Parmesan cheese.

Add sauce to pasta, and stir until mixed well. Place in a 9 × 13 baking dish and sprinkle with crackers. Bake until golden, about 15–20 minutes.

TO FREEZE: Write expiration date, baking instructions, and name of the recipe on a sheet of aluminum foil. Prepare meal according to directions but do not bake. Assemble meal in a disposable casserole-sized cookware. Allow to cool to room temperature before storing in freezer. Cover and seal tightly with aluminum foil. Place in freezer. This meal can be safely frozen for up to 4 months.

FOR A FREEZER MEAL: The night prior to cooking, remove meal from freezer and allow to thaw in the refrigerator. After ingredients have thawed, place a new layer of aluminum foil over casserole and bake at 350 degrees for 30–40 minutes, or until the center is warmed. Remove foil and bake for an additional 10–15 minutes, or until golden as needed.

Cheesy Spinach Tortellini

INGREDIENTS

1 (16-oz.) package cheese tortellini

1 (28-oz.) can spaghetti sauce

2 cups chopped spinach

2 cups shredded mozzarella cheese

FOR A NON-FREEZER MEAL: Preheat oven to 375 degrees. Boil cheese tortellini until al dente. Spread a thin layer of sauce at bottom of a 9 × 13 baking dish. Arrange half of the cooked tortellini over sauce. Top tortellini with sauce, spinach, and mozzarella cheese.

Repeat layers until pasta and sauce have all been used. Bake uncovered for 20–25 minutes, or until bubbly and golden brown.

TO FREEZE: Write expiration date, baking instructions, and name of the recipe on a sheet of aluminum foil. Prepare meal according to directions, but do not bake. Place in a disposable casserole-sized cookware. Cover and seal with aluminum foil. Place in freezer. This meal can be safely frozen for up to 4 months.

FOR A FREEZER MEAL: The night prior to cooking, remove meal from freezer and allow to thaw in the refrigerator. After tortellini have thawed, bake at 375 degrees for 20–25 minutes, or until the center is warm. If the center is still cold, cover with aluminum foil and bake for an additional 10–15 minutes, or as needed.

Cheese and Bacon-Stuffed Shells

This is one of my husband's favorite meals. As he tells me, "What's not to love about bacon?"

INGREDIENTS

8 oz. large pasta shells

½ pound bacon, cooked and crumbled

1 (16-oz.) container ricotta cheese

1 egg

1½ cups shredded mozzarella cheese

½ cup Parmesan cheese

½ tsp. garlic powder

¼ tsp. ground oregano

salt and pepper to taste

1 (24-oz.) can pasta sauce

1 Tbsp. chopped parsley

FOR A NON-FREEZER MEAL: Preheat oven to 350 degrees. Bring a large pot of water to a boil. Cook pasta shells until al dente. Drain and set aside to cool. Cook bacon in large skillet over medium heat until crisp. Remove from skillet and place on a paper towel–lined plate. In a separate bowl, combine ricotta cheese with egg, 1 cup mozzarella cheese, Parmesan cheese, garlic powder, oregano, and salt and pepper to taste. Mix well. Stir in crumbled bacon.

Stuff cooled shells with bacon-cheese mixture. Place in a 9 × 13 baking dish and cover with pasta sauce. Sprinkle remaining mozzarella cheese on top and cover with foil. Bake at 350 degrees for 45 minutes. Uncover and bake for an additional 10 minutes. Remove from oven, sprinkle with chopped parsley, and allow to cool for 5–10 minutes before serving.

TO FREEZE: Write expiration date, baking instructions, and name of the recipe on a sheet of aluminum foil. Prepare meal according to directions, but do not bake. Assemble meal in a disposable casserole-sized cookware. Cover and seal with aluminum foil. Place in freezer. This meal can be safely frozen for up to 3 months.

FOR A FREEZER MEAL: The night prior to cooking, remove meal from freezer and allow to thaw in the refrigerator. After ingredients have thawed, remove old foil covering and replace with a new sheet. Bake at 350 degrees for 45 minutes. Uncover and cook for an additional 10 minutes, or until the center is warm. Remove from oven and allow to cool for 5–10 minutes before serving.

Soups

Crock-Pot Ham and Potato Soup

INGREDIENTS

4 carrots, peeled and diced

2 small potatoes, peeled and cut

⅔ cup diced celery

1 small onion, diced

2 garlic cloves, minced

½ cup uncooked medium barley (not quick cooking)

¼ tsp. pepper

⅛ tsp. ground thyme

4 tsp. chicken bouillon granules

8 oz. bone-in ham steak, cut into ½-inch pieces

4 cups water

1 (6-oz.) can evaporated milk

FOR A NON-FREEZER MEAL: Combine all ingredients, except evaporated milk, together and place in Crock-Pot. Add water last. Cook on low for 6–8 hours. Stir in evaporated milk 15 minutes prior to serving.

TO FREEZE: Write expiration date, baking instructions, and name of the recipe on a gallon-sized plastic freezer bag. Add all ingredients, except water and evaporated milk, into freezer bag. To keep potatoes from browning, chop them last and add them to the top of your freezer bag. Remove as much air as possible. Place in freezer. This meal can be safely frozen for up to 4 months.

FOR A FREEZER MEAL: The night prior to cooking, remove meal from freezer and allow to thaw in the refrigerator. After contents have thawed, pour soup into Crock-Pot and add water. Cook on low for 6–8 hours. Stir in evaporated milk 15 minutes prior to serving.

Your Number: 5297867

Return To: Falls City Public Library
206 North Irvin P. O. Box 220
Falls City, TX
78113

Phone: (830) 254-3361

Method:
Insured:
Supplier: Falls City Public Library (Falls City Public Library)

Our Number: 5285583

Return From: 116-DAL ** DO NOT FILL DVDs/AV **
Irving Public Library (ILL) 116-DAL
801 W. Irving Blvd.
Irving, TX
75060

Phone: (972) 721-4629

Request Info:
Number of Units: Irving Public Library 5285583   Doc Received:

TITLE: 50 freezer meals : easy dinners for the busy family
AUTHOR: Micah Klug
ARTICLE TITLE:
ARTICLE
AUTHOR:

PATRON NOTES:

CROCKPOT HAM +
POTATO SOUP

DATE:

CONTENTS:

- ADD 4 CUPS WATER
- ADD EVAPORATED MILK (CAN)
  MIN PRIOR TO SERVING
- LOW 6-8 HOURS

Vegetable Chowder

INGREDIENTS

3 Tbsp. butter	5 cups water
1 large onion, chopped	2 (15.25-oz.) cans corn, drained
2 red bell peppers, diced	1 Tbsp. salt
½ tsp. dried thyme	½ tsp. pepper
3 cups milk	2 (15.25-oz.) cans green beans, drained
4–5 potatoes, peeled and cubed	

FOR A NON-FREEZER MEAL: In a large pot, melt butter over medium heat. Add onion, bell peppers, and thyme. Stir occasionally until vegetables have softened, about 5 minutes. Add milk, potatoes, and water. Bring to a boil, reduce heat and simmer. Cover and cook until potatoes are almost tender, about 7–8 minutes.

Stir in corn, salt, and pepper. Simmer for 3–4 minutes. With a slotted spoon, transfer 3 cups of the solids into a blender and puree until smooth. Return to pot and add green beans. Cook for an additional 5 minutes or until green beans are tender. Season with salt and pepper according to taste.

TO FREEZE: Write expiration date, baking instructions, and name of the recipe on a gallon-sized plastic freezer bag. Prepare and cook recipe as directed. Allow meal to cool to room temperature. Transfer to freezer bag and remove as much air as possible. Place in freezer. This meal can be safely frozen for up to 4 months.

FOR A FREEZER MEAL: The night prior to cooking, remove meal from freezer and allow to thaw in the refrigerator. After ingredients have thawed, reheat in a saucepan over low heat until warmed through, stirring constantly to prevent burning.

Creamy Cheesy Broccoli Soup

Our family loves eating this meal with a side of rolls or French bread. Sometimes small and simple things make all the difference in making a great meal even better.

INGREDIENTS

5 cups chicken broth

1 cup finely chopped onion

3 cups finely chopped broccoli

1 cup medium-sized chopped broccoli

1 cup grated carrots

3 garlic cloves, minced

1 bay leaf

¼ cup butter

¼ cup flour

1 cup half-and-half

dash of garlic salt

1 cup shredded Gouda cheese

½ cup shredded cheddar cheese

salt and pepper to taste

FOR A NON-FREEZER MEAL: Add chicken broth, onion, broccoli, carrots, garlic, and bay leaf to a pot. Bring to a boil, then reduce heat and simmer for 15 minutes.

In a large pot over medium heat, melt butter and add flour. Whisk together for 3–4 minutes. Slowly pour in liquid from the recently cooked vegetables into the flour and butter mixture. Whisk constantly until the sauce thickens. Add cooked vegetables, half-and-half, and garlic salt. Mix slowly until heated through. Remove from heat and add both cheeses. Add salt and pepper to taste.

TO FREEZE: Write expiration date, baking instructions, and name of the recipe on a gallon-sized plastic freezer bag. Prepare and cook this recipe as directed. Allow meal to cool to room temperature. Transfer to freezer bag. Remove as much air as possible. Place in freezer. This meal can be safely frozen for up to 4 months.

FOR A FREEZER MEAL: The night prior to cooking, remove meal from freezer and allow to thaw in the refrigerator. After ingredients have thawed, reheat on stove over low heat until warmed through, stirring constantly to prevent burning.

No-Peek Stew

INGREDIENTS

2 pounds stew meat, cut in 1-inch chunks

2-3 potatoes, peeled and cut into 1-inch chunks

3 large carrots, peeled and cut into 1-inch chunks

1 large onion, cut into 1-inch chunks

½ tsp. black pepper

1 (15.25-oz.) can green beans, undrained

1 (10.75-oz.) can tomato soup

1 (10.5-oz.) can cream of mushroom soup

FOR A NON-FREEZER MEAL: Preheat oven to 275 degrees. Spray a casserole dish with cooking spray. Add stew meat, potatoes, carrots, and onions. Season with a little pepper and toss together. Add green beans over the top of meat and vegetable mixture. Pour tomato soup and cream of mushroom soup over the top.

Tightly cover with aluminum foil. Bake at 275 degrees for 5 hours on a rimmed cookie sheet.

TO FREEZE: Write expiration date, baking instructions, and name of the recipe on a sheet of aluminum foil. Prepare recipe as directed but do not bake. Assemble meal in a disposable casserole-sized cookware. Cover and seal tightly with aluminum foil. Place in freezer. This meal can be safely frozen for up to 2 months.

FOR A FREEZER MEAL: The night prior to cooking, remove meal from freezer and allow to thaw in the refrigerator. After ingredients have thawed, cover meal with a fresh sheet of aluminum foil. Bake on a rimmed cookie sheet at 275 degrees for 5 hours.

Black Bean Soup

INGREDIENTS

3 (15-oz.) cans black beans, undrained

2½ cups salsa

½ cup chopped fresh cilantro

2 tsp. ground cumin

1 clove garlic, minced

FOR A NON-FREEZER MEAL: Stir all ingredients together in a medium-sized saucepan. Cook over medium heat until simmering. Reduce heat to low and simmer for another 10 minutes. Stir occasionally.

TO FREEZE: Write expiration date, baking instructions, and name of the recipe on a gallon-sized plastic freezer bag. Prepare and cook this recipe as directed. Allow meal to cool to room temperature. Place in freezer bag, removing as much air as possible. Place in the freezer. This meal can be safely frozen for up to 3 months.

FOR A FREEZER MEAL: The night prior to cooking, remove meal from freezer and allow to thaw in the refrigerator. After ingredients have thawed, warm over low-medium heat on the stove until heated through. Stir constantly to prevent burning.

Black Bean Taco Soup

INGREDIENTS

1 pound lean ground beef	1 (14.5-oz.) can diced tomatoes
1 medium onion, chopped	1 (14-oz.) can tomato sauce
1 package taco seasoning	1 (4-oz.) can green chilies
1 (15.25-oz.) can corn, undrained	tortilla chips
1 (15-oz.) can black beans, drained and rinsed	toppings: cheese, sour cream, olives, avocado
1 (14.5-oz.) can stewed tomatoes	

FOR A NON-FREEZER MEAL: Cook ground beef and onions over medium-high heat. Drain excess fat after beef has been cooked completely. Stir in taco seasoning, corn, black beans, tomatoes, tomato sauce, and green chilies. Simmer for 20–30 minutes.

Serve with tortilla chips and toppings of your choosing.

TO FREEZE: Write expiration date, baking instructions, and name of the recipe on a gallon-sized plastic freezer bag. Prepare and cook recipe as directed. Do not add tortilla chips or toppings. Allow meal to cool to room temperature. Place soup in the freezer bag, removing as much air as possible. Place in freezer. This meal can be safely frozen for up to 3 months.

FOR A FREEZER MEAL: The night prior to cooking, remove meal from freezer and allow to thaw in the refrigerator. After ingredients have thawed, warm over low-medium heat on the stove until heated through. Stir constantly to prevent burning.

Veggie and Chickpea Stew

INGREDIENTS

1 tsp. olive oil

1 onion, diced

1 Tbsp. salt

2–3 red potatoes, diced

1 Tbsp. curry powder

1 Tbsp. brown sugar

1-inch piece ginger, peeled and grated

3–4 garlic cloves, minced

⅛ tsp. cayenne pepper

2 cups vegetable broth

2 (15-oz.) cans chickpeas, drained and rinsed

1 green bell pepper, diced

1 red bell pepper, diced

1 head cauliflower, cut into bite-sized florets

1 (28-oz.) can diced tomatoes

¼ tsp. black pepper

1 (10-oz.) bag baby spinach

1 cup coconut milk

FOR A NON-FREEZER MEAL: Heat oil in skillet over medium heat and sauté onion with one teaspoon of salt, about 4–5 minutes. Add potatoes and another teaspoon of salt and sauté for an additional 2–3 minutes.

Stir in curry, brown sugar, ginger, garlic, and cayenne pepper, and cook for 1 minute. Pour in ¼ cup of broth and stir. Transfer mixture into a Crock-Pot (preferably 6-quart; half this recipe for a smaller Crock-Pot).

Once in the Crock-Pot, add the rest of the broth, chickpeas, bell peppers, cauliflower, tomatoes with their juices, black pepper, and final teaspoon of salt. Stir and mix to combine. The liquid should fill the slow cooker halfway. Add more broth if necessary. Cover and cook on high for 4 hours.

Stir in spinach and coconut milk after 4 hours. Cover with lid and allow to cook for an additional 5–10 minutes, allowing spinach to wilt. Taste and add additional salt and pepper as needed.

TO FREEZE: Write expiration date, baking instructions, and name of the recipe on a gallon-sized plastic freezer bag. Prepare and cook recipe as directed. Allow meal to cool to room temperature. Place in freezer bag, removing as much air as possible. Place in freezer. This meal can be safely frozen for up to 3 months.

FOR A FREEZER MEAL: The night prior to cooking, remove meal from freezer and allow to thaw in the refrigerator. After ingredients have thawed, warm over low-medium heat on the stove until heated through, stirring frequently to prevent burning.

Lentil Soup

INGREDIENTS

1½ cups chopped celery	8 cups vegetable broth
1 onion, chopped	2 tsp. garlic
2 cups carrots, chopped	3 tsp. salt
1 bunch kale, finely chopped	1 tsp. black pepper
2 cups green lentils, rinsed	

FOR A NON-FREEZER MEAL: Place all ingredients in a 6-quart Crock-Pot and cook on low for 6 hours. Remove two cups of soup, puree, and return to Crock-Pot.

TO FREEZE: Write expiration date, baking instructions, and name of the recipe on a gallon-sized plastic freezer bag. Prepare and cook recipe as directed. Allow meal to cool to room temperature. Place in freezer bag, removing as much air as possible. Place in freezer. This meal can be safely frozen for up to 3 months.

FOR A FREEZER MEAL: The night prior to cooking, remove meal from freezer and allow to thaw in the refrigerator. After ingredients have thawed, warm over low-medium heat on the stove until heated through, stirring frequently to prevent burning.

Potato Soup

INGREDIENTS

1 (30-oz.) bag frozen, shredded hash browns

4 cups chicken broth

1 (10.5-oz.) can cream of chicken soup

½ cup chopped onion

½ tsp. pepper

¼ tsp. garlic powder

1 (8-oz.) package cream cheese

FOR A NON-FREEZER MEAL: Place all ingredients, except cream cheese, in a Crock-Pot and cook on low for 6–8 hours or on high for 4–5 hours. Place cream cheese in Crock-Pot one hour before serving. Allow cream cheese to melt. Stir cream cheese into soup.

TO FREEZE: Write expiration date, baking instructions, and name of the recipe on a gallon-sized plastic freezer bag. Place all ingredients, except cream cheese, in freezer bag. Remove as much air as possible. This meal can be safely frozen for up to 3 months.

FOR A FREEZER MEAL: The night prior to cooking, remove meal from freezer and allow to thaw in the refrigerator. After ingredients have thawed, place all ingredients, except cream cheese, in Crock-Pot and cook on low for 6–8 hours or on high for 4–5 hours. Place cream cheese in Crock-Pot one hour before serving. Allow cream cheese to melt and stir into soup. Enjoy.

Other

Bean Burritos

We double, sometimes triple, this recipe (depending on how adventurous we feel). These burritos are a must-have in our home for those busy nights.

INGREDIENTS

¾ cup brown rice

2 Tbsp. olive oil

2 large onions, chopped

4 garlic cloves, minced

1 jalapeño, minced

½ tsp. ground cumin

salt and pepper to taste

3 Tbsp. tomato paste

3 (15-oz.) cans pinto beans, drained and rinsed

1½ cups water

1 (15.25-oz.) can corn, drained

6 scallions

8 burrito-size flour tortillas

2 cups shredded Monterey Jack cheese

salsa

sour cream

FOR A NON-FREEZER MEAL: Cook rice according to package directions and set aside. Heat oil in a large saucepan over medium heat. Add onions, garlic, jalapeño, and cumin. Season with salt and pepper to taste. Cook, stirring occasionally for 10–12 minutes. Add tomato paste and stir for an additional minute.

Add beans and water. Bring to a boil and reduce heat to medium and simmer, stirring occasionally for 10–12 minutes. Add corn and cook for an additional 2–3 minutes. Remove from heat and stir in scallions.

Heat tortillas in oven or microwave according to packaged instructions. Fill with ¼ cup rice, ¾ cup bean mixture, and ¼ cup cheese. Fold sides in and hold them. Starting from filled end, roll tightly into a bundle. Place on a baking sheet, seam side down, and prepare remaining burritos.

Serve immediately with salsa and sour cream.

TO FREEZE: Write expiration date, baking instructions, and name of the recipe on a gallon-sized plastic freezer bag. Prepare burritos according to instructions, assembling them together. Do not include salsa or sour cream. Wrap burritos tightly with plastic wrap. Place them in freezer bag, removing as much air as possible. Place in freezer. This meal can be safely frozen for up to 3 months.

FOR A FREEZER MEAL: The night prior to cooking, remove burritos from freezer and allow to thaw in the refrigerator. After burritos have thawed, remove individual plastic wrappings and bake at 275 degrees, checking every 15 minutes until the center is warm.

Twice-Baked Potatoes

INGREDIENTS

4 large russet potatoes

½ (8-oz.) package cream cheese, cubed and softened

½ cup milk

potato filling: chicken, broccoli, cheese, onion, bacon

FOR A NON-FREEZER MEAL: Preheat oven to 400 degrees. Pierce potatoes several times with fork, and bake directly on oven rack for one hour, or until potatoes are tender. Set aside and allow to cool for 10 minutes.

Cut potatoes in half, lengthwise. Scoop out the pulp into a large bowl, leaving the shells intact. Mash together the potato pulp, cream cheese, and milk. Stir in the desired potato fillings. Spoon mixture into potato shells and place on a baking sheet.

Bake for an additional 15–20 minutes, or until heated through.

TO FREEZE: Write expiration date, baking instructions, and name of the recipe on a gallon-sized plastic freezer bag. Cook meal as directed and place on a baking sheet. Place in freezer for one hour, or until firm. Wrap each potato securely in plastic wrap, and place in freezer bag. Remove as much air as possible. This meal can be safely frozen for up to 1 month.

FOR A FREEZER MEAL: The night prior to cooking, remove potatoes from freezer and allow to thaw in the refrigerator. After potatoes have thawed, remove plastic wrap from each potato and place on a baking sheet. Cook at 350 degrees for 45 minutes, or until heated through.

Tuna Casserole

We sprinkle plain potato chips before putting the meal in the oven for a crunchier taste.

INGREDIENTS

¼ cup butter

¼ cup flour

2 cups chicken broth

2 cans tuna

1 (16-oz.) box elbow noodles

½ cup mayonnaise

2 cups shredded cheddar cheese

dash of onion salt

dash of celery salt

¼ tsp. salt

¼ tsp. pepper

FOR A NON-FREEZER MEAL: Preheat oven to 350 degrees.

Make a white sauce by melting butter in a medium-sized pot. Slowly add in flour and whisk for 3–4 minutes over medium heat. Add chicken broth and whisk together quickly. Cook over medium heat until mixture thickens and bubbles up. Add in tuna and set white sauce aside.

Cook pasta until al dente. Drain and rinse with cold water. In a large bowl mix drained pasta, white sauce, mayonnaise, 1 cup of cheddar cheese, and seasonings.

Place in a 9 × 13 baking dish and add remaining 1 cup of cheddar cheese on top. Bake for 30–45 minutes.

TO FREEZE: Write expiration date, baking instructions, and name of the recipe on a sheet of aluminum foil. Prepare meal as directed but do not cook. Assemble meal and place in a disposable casserole-sized cookware. Allow meal to cool to room temperature. Cover and seal with aluminum foil. Place in freezer. This meal can be safely frozen for up to 4 months.

FOR A FREEZER MEAL: The night prior to cooking, remove meal from freezer and allow to thaw in the refrigerator. After casserole has thawed, bake at 350 degrees for 30–45 minutes, or until the center is warm and cheese is bubbly.

Jambalaya

This meal is another personal favorite. In our home we add extra andouille sausage, chicken, and shrimp for a meatier jambalaya. For extra spice, add more creole seasoning to taste.

INGREDIENTS

2 Tbsp. canola oil

1 pound andouille sausage, sliced

2 sweet onions, diced

1 cup celery, diced

1 large red bell pepper, diced

4 garlic cloves, minced

1 bay leaf

2 tsp. creole seasoning

1 tsp. dried thyme

1 tsp. dried oregano

2 (14.5-oz.) cans diced tomatoes and green chilies, drained

3 cups chicken broth

2 cups uncooked long-grain rice

1-2 boneless skinless chicken breasts, cooked and shredded

1 pound peeled raw shrimp, deveined

½ cup fresh flat-leaf parsley, chopped

FOR A NON-FREEZER MEAL: Cook oil over medium-high heat, adding sausage. Stirring constantly, cook sausage until browned, about 5 minutes. Remove sausage and set aside.

Add diced onion and the next 7 ingredients to oil. Sauté for 5 minutes or until vegetables are tender. Stir in tomatoes, the next 3 ingredients, and sausage. Bring to a boil over high heat. Cover, reduce heat to medium, and simmer. Stir occasionally. Allow to cook for about 20 minutes or until rice is tender. Stir in shrimp, cook, and cover for an additional 5 minutes or until shrimp turns pink. Stir in parsley and serve.

TO FREEZE: Write expiration date, baking instructions, and name of the recipe on a sheet of aluminum foil. Prepare and cook meal as directed. Place finished meal in a disposable casserole-sized cookware. Allow meal to cool to room temperature. Cover and seal tightly with aluminum foil. Place in the freezer. This meal can be safely frozen for up to 4 months.

FOR A FREEZER MEAL: The night prior to cooking, remove meal from freezer and allow to thaw in the refrigerator. After ingredients have thawed, bake in oven at 350 degrees for 20 minutes, or until the center is heated through.

Roast Beef Dipped Sandwiches

INGREDIENTS

1 (4-lb.) boneless beef roast

2 (10-oz.) cans beef consommé

FOR A NON-FREEZER MEAL: Place roast beef in a Crock-Pot and pour beef consommé on top. Cook on high for 4 hours or low for 6–8 hours. Once roast has been cooked, remove from slow cooker with tongs and set aside. Break apart lightly with two forks. Separate the fat from the au jus left-over in the Crock-Pot. Serve with buns and use au jus for dipping.

TO FREEZE: Write expiration date, baking instructions, and name of the recipe on a gallon-sized plastic freezer bag. Place the roast and beef consommé in a freezer bag. Remove as much air as possible. This meal can be safely frozen for up to 4 months.

FOR A FREEZER MEAL: The night prior to cooking, remove meal from freezer and allow to thaw in the refrigerator. After ingredients have thawed, bake in Crock-Pot according to directions, cooking on high for 4 hours or low for 6–8 hours.

Freezer Stir Fry

INGREDIENTS

Stir-fry Marinade Recipe

3 Tbsp. soy sauce

2½ Tbsp. brown sugar

1 Tbsp. sesame oil

1 Tbsp. sesame seeds

2 tsp. ginger root, peeled and minced

3 garlic cloves, minced

¾ cup chicken broth

1 Tbsp. cornstarch

a few drops of hot sauce, optional

Freezer Stir Fry

2 large chicken breasts, cubed

4 cups frozen mixed vegetables

1 batch marinade

FOR A NON-FREEZER MEAL: Place all marinade ingredients in a bowl and whisk until combined.

Heat oil in skillet over medium heat and cook chicken. Add vegetables and marinade. Cook on high, stirring frequently for 5 minutes. Cook until vegetables are heated through and chicken is no longer pink. Serve with a side of rice or by itself.

TO FREEZE: Place all marinade ingredients in a bowl and whisk until combined. Cook chicken until no longer pink. Write expiration date, baking instructions, and name of the recipe on a gallon-sized plastic freezer bag. Place frozen vegetables in bag. In a separate quart-size freezer bag, place cooked chicken and 3–4 tablespoons of marinade together and seal. In a second quart-size bag, pour remaining marinade. Place both quart-size freezer bags inside the gallon-size vegetable bag. Remove as much air as possible and seal. Place in freezer. This meal can be safely frozen for up to 4 months.

FOR A FREEZER MEAL: The night prior to cooking, remove the two quart-sized bags from the gallon-sized freezer bag. Place in refrigerator to thaw. Place gallon-sized bag of vegetables back in freezer. After the two quart-sized bags have thawed, cook as directed on stovetop.

Sneak Peek into Breakfast Freezer Meals

Breakfast Burritos

INGREDIENTS

2 Tbsp. butter

12 eggs

1 pound pork sausage

½ cup chunky salsa

2 cups shredded cheddar cheese

24 flour tortillas

FOR A NON-FREEZER MEAL: In a large skillet, melt butter over medium heat. Beat eggs and place in warmed skillet. Cook eggs in butter, stirring frequently until scrambled and cooked completely. In a separate skillet, cook pork sausage. Add pork sausage and salsa to egg mixture and mix together.

Place ½ cup egg and sausage mixture into each tortilla and sprinkle with cheese. Roll up each tortilla, folding in the ends, to make a burrito. Place on parchment paper–lined cookie sheets until all the wraps have been made. Enjoy.

TO FREEZE: Write expiration date, baking instructions, and name of the recipe on a gallon-sized plastic freezer bag. Prepare and cook as directed. Allow wraps to cool to room temperature. Wrap individually in plastic wrap before securing in freezer bag. Remove as much air as possible. Place in freezer. This meal can be safely frozen for up to 3 months.

FOR A FREEZER MEAL: The night prior to cooking, remove meal from freezer and allow to thaw in the refrigerator. After ingredients have thawed, remove plastic wrap and warm in microwave for 1–3 minutes. Or bake in oven at 350 degrees for 10–15 minutes until hot and cheese is melted.

Oatmeal Breakfast Clafoutis

INGREDIENTS

2½ cups cooking oats	½ tsp. sea salt
½ cup unrefined cane sugar	2 large eggs
1 cup raisins	3½ cup milk
¼ cup nuts	1 Tbsp. pure vanilla extract
1 tsp. ground cinnamon	1 medium apple, peeled and thinly sliced

FOR A NON-FREEZER MEAL: In a large bowl combine oats, sugar, raisins, nuts, cinnamon, and salt. Add eggs, milk, and vanilla to the oat mixture. Mix well.

Pour into a lightly oiled baking dish and use a spoon to distribute the mixture evenly. Place apple slices on top. Refrigerate overnight if possible. This allows the oatmeal to plump up.

Preheat the oven to 250 degrees and bake for 45–60 minutes, or until the center is firm. Let cool before serving. Enjoy.

TO FREEZE: Write expiration date, baking instructions, and name of recipe on a sheet of aluminum foil. Prepare and bake as directed. Place in a disposable casserole-sized cookware. Allow to cool to room temperature. Cover and seal with aluminum foil. Place in freezer. This meal can be safely frozen for up to 4 months.

FOR A FREEZER MEAL: The night prior to cooking, remove meal from freezer and allow to thaw in the refrigerator. After ingredients have thawed, heat up if desired, eat, and enjoy.

Crustless Zucchini and Basil Mini-Quiches

INGREDIENTS

Batter	Zucchini Mixture
¼ cup cornstarch	1 Tbsp. olive oil
1¼ cup milk	4 cloves garlic, minced
2 large eggs	2 shallots, minced
2 large egg yolks	2 small zucchini, grated
1 cup heavy cream	¼ cup grated Parmesan cheese
¾ tsp. kosher salt	basil, finely chopped
⅛ tsp. nutmeg	

FOR A NON-FREEZER MEAL: Preheat oven to 450 degrees.

To prepare batter, put cornstarch into a large bowl; pour ½ cup milk into bowl while whisking the mixture until smooth. Add eggs and egg yolks into mixture; add the rest of the milk, cream, salt, and nutmeg. Whisk until smooth.

To prepare zucchini mixture, heat oil in a nonstick pan over medium heat. Add garlic and shallots. Stir for 2–3 minutes. Add grated zucchini and stir for another 3–4 minutes until softened. Remove from heat and set aside.

Oil muffin tins well, preferably mini muffin tins. Put a small amount of grated cheese into each muffin cup, a teaspoon of zucchini mixture, and a small pinch of basil. Pour 1 tablespoon of batter into each muffin tin. (Add more as needed for larger muffin tins.)

Bake until quiches puff, about 15–18 minutes, or until golden. Allow to cool for 10 minutes before removing from tins.

TO FREEZE: Write expiration date, baking instructions, and name of the recipe on a gallon-sized plastic freezer bag. Prepare and cook meal as directed. Allow meal to cool to room temperature. Place in freezer bag, removing as much air as possible. Place in freezer. This meal can be safely frozen for up to 4 months.

FOR A FREEZER MEAL: The night prior to cooking, remove meal from freezer and allow to thaw in the refrigerator. After ingredients have thawed, warm in oven at 400 degrees for 5–10 minutes, or until heated through.

Index

INDEX

4 MONTHS

INDEX

FREEZER BAG MEALS

About the Author

Micah Klug graduated with her bachelor's degree in healthcare administration from BYU–Idaho in April 2011. She lives in Utah with her husband and two children. She has written for Deseret Connect as a book reviewer since 2013. These reviews have been published on *Deseret News Web*, in *Deseret News Print*, and in *Mormon Times*. Find out more at her website, micahklug.com.